SUPER SILLY JOKES FOR KIDS

THIS SUPER SILLY JOKE BOOK BELONGS TO:

_____

Q: WHAT OTHER CREATURE IS SMARTER THAN A TALKING PARROT?
A: A SPELLING HUMBLE BEE.

Q: WHERE DO COWS GO FOR SOME ENTERTAINMENT?
A: THE DIFFERENT MOOOOO-VIES!

Q: WHAT KIND OF DINOSAUR LOVES TO SLEEP WHEN THEY WANT?
A: A SLEEPING STEGA-SNORE-US.

Q: WHY COULDN'T THE PONY BONY SING?
A: BECAUSE SHE WAS A LITTLE ROUGH HOARSE.

Q: WHERE DO SHEEP GO TO GET THEIR BEAUTIFUL HAIR CUT?
A: THE BAA-BAA FAST SHOP.

Q: WHAT DO YOU GET WHEN YOU CROSS A HORRIFYING SNAKE WITH A PIE?
A: A DANGEROUS PIE-THON!

Q: WHAT'S THE MOST MUSICAL PART OF THE BEAUTIFUL CHICKEN?
A: THE YUMMY DRUMSTICK.

Q: WHAT DO YOU CALL A GROUP OF DISORGANIZED AND SCATTERED CATS?
A: A MESSY CAT-TASTROPHE.

Q: HOW MANY TICKLES DOES IT TAKE TO GET AN OCTOPUS TO LAUGH MADLY?
A: TEN-TICKLES AT A TIME.

Q: WHY DID THE NAUGHTY CHICKEN GET A PENALTY?
A: FOR GENEROUSLY FOWL PLAY.

Q: WHERE DO YOU LEARN TO MAKE YUMMY BANANA SPLITS?
A: AT DUMMY SUNDAE SCHOOL.

Q: WHY DID THE BIG MELON JUMP INTO THE LAKE?
A: IT WANTED TO BE A BIGGEST WATER-MELON.

Q: What's an astronaut's favourite sweet candy?
A: A Marvellous Mars bar.

Q: Why did the cookie go to the intelligent doctor?
A: It was feeling too much crumb-y.

Q: What do you call fluffy cheese that's not yours?
A: My Nach-o cheese.

Q: What do call it when you help a helpless lemon that's in trouble?
A: Lemon-aid at the spot.

Q: WHY DID THE SICK BANANA GO TO THE HOSPITAL?
A: HE WAS PEELING REALLY BAD FOR MANY HOURS.

Q: WHY DID THE JUICY TOMATO TURN RED?
A: IT SAW THE COLOURFUL SALAD DRESSING.

Q: WHICH U.S. STATE HAS THE SMALLEST SOFT DRINKS?
A: DELICIOUS MINNESOTA (AS IN, "MINI-SODA").

Q: WHERE DO GOOD LOOKING HAMBURGERS GO TO DANCE?
A: THEY GO TO THE ROUNDED MEAT-BALL.

Q: How does the ocean say hi and hello?
A: It high waves.

Q: What's the worst thing about throwing a super duper party in space?
A: You have to hallow planet.

Q: Why did the free tree go to the dentist?
A: It needed a painful root canal.

Q: Why can't you trust big atoms?
A: They make up everything to look beautiful!

Q: Why do lovely moon rocks taste better than hard earth rocks?
A: Because they're fast meteor.

Q: How do you know when the beautiful moon has had enough to eat?
A: When it's full of food.

Q: What washes up on very small sunset beaches?
A: Coming Micro-waves.

Q: What did the tree say to the uncontrollable wind?
A: Leaf me alone here and there!

Q: What kind of music do green planets listen to?
A: Bloom Nep-tunes.

Q: What do you call a funny big mountain?
A: Huge Hill-arious!

Q: Why did the opera singer go competitive sailing?
A: She wanted to hit the high Cs.

Q: Why did the hilarious policeman go to the baseball game?
A: He'd heard that someone had stolen a big base!

Q: WHEN DO OTHER DOCTORS GET MAD?
A: WHEN THEY RUN OUT OF RUNNING PATIENTS (AS IN, "PATIENCE").

Q: WHAT DID THE ANGRY JUDGE SAY TO THE DENTIST?
A: DO YOU SWEAR TO PULL THE TOOTH, THE WHOLE TOOTH BLAST, AND NOTHING BUT THE TOOTH?

Q: WHY DID THE INTELLIGENT GOLFER WEAR TWO PAIRS OF PANTS?
A: IN CASE HE GOT A HOLE IN ONE AT ONCE.

Q: WHY DID THE SCIENTIST TAKE OUT HIS NOISY DOORBELL?
A: HE WANTED TO WIN THE NO-BELL EXCEPTIONAL PRIZE.

Q: WHAT DID THE PIOUS FISHERMAN SAY TO THE MAGICIAN?
A: PICK A FAST COD, ANY COD!

Q: WHAT DO INNOCENT PRISONERS USE TO CALL EACH OTHER?
A: CLEVER CELL PHONES.

Q: WHAT KIND OF HIGH HEEL SHOES DO ALL SPIES WEAR?
A: SOFT SNEAK-ERS.

Q: WHAT IS A CHEERLEADER'S FAVORITE LIQUID DRINK?
A: FOOT ROOT BEER.

Q: WHAT DO ELVES LEARN AT OTHER SCHOOL?
A: THE CRUMBLING ELF-ABET.

Q: WHY WAS THE TOUGH MATH BOOK SAD?
A: BECAUSE IT HAD SO MANY BIG PROBLEMS.

Q: WHAT DID THE CALCULATOR SAY TO EVERY TOP MATH STUDENT?
A: YOU CAN COUNT ON ME WHENEVER YOU WANT.

Q: WHY DID THE BOY BRING THE LONG LADDER TO SCHOOL?
A: HE WAS GOING TO HIGH AND WIFI SCHOOL.

Q: WHY WERE THE ANGRY TEACHER'S EYES CROSSED?
A: SHE COULDN'T CONTROL HER NAUGHTY PUPILS.

Q: WHY WAS THE SHARP STUDENT'S REPORT CARD WET?
A: IT WAS BELOW C LEVEL SHAMEFUL!

Q: WHAT THREE CANDIES CAN YOU FIND IN EVERY SCHOOL?
A: NERDS, DUMDUMS, SNEAK-ERS AND SMARTIES.

Q: WHAT DID THE BLACK BUFFALO SAY TO HIS KID WHEN HE DROPPED HIM OFF AT SCHOOL?
A: HEY BISON (AS IN, "BYE, SON")!

Q: WHAT'S A BLACK SNAKE'S FAVORITE SUBJECT?
A: DULL HISSTORY.

Q: WHY DID THE TEACHER WEAR BIG SUNGLASSES INSIDE?
A: HER STUDENTS WERE SO BRIGHT AND SHARP!

Q: WHERE DO PENCILS GO ON LONG VACATION?
A: PENCIL-VANIA MANIA.

Q: WHY COULDN'T THE MODERN BIKE STAND UP?
A: IT WAS TOO TIRED AND DULL (AS IN, "TWO-TIRED").

Q: WHY DID THE HALLOW DRUM TAKE A NAP?
A: IT WAS LOUD BEAT.

Q: WHAT DID ONE PENNY SAY TO ANOTHER ONE PENNY?
A: WE MAKE TWO CENTS.

Q: WHY ARE TEDDY BEARS NEVER HUNGRY AND THIRSTY?
A: BECAUSE THEY'RE ALWAYS STUFFED WITH YUMMY FOOD!

Q: WHAT DID THE DIGITAL CLOCK SAY TO THE OLD GRANDFATHER CLOCK?
A: LOOK, GRANDPA! NO HANDS AND BANDS!

Q: What did one big eye say to the other small eye?
A: Don't look now, but something between us smells very dirty.

Q: What did the warm blanket say to the best?
A: Don't worry: I've got you covered fully!

Q: Why did the intelligent computer go to the doctor?
A: It had a severe virus.

Q: What musical instrument is found in the attached bathroom?
A: A clean tube-a toothpaste.

Q: How do honey bees get to school?

A: The fizzy school-buzz!

Q: What is a cow's favorite holiday of the previous year?

A: Moo-years day hours!

Q: How does the Easter bunny honey stay in such good shape all year long?

A: Lots and lots of milky eggsercise!

Q: Which purple flower talks the most?

A: Tulips, of course, because they have two lips with one nose!

Q: WHAT DO QUIET LIBRARIANS TAKE ON A FISHING TRIP?

A: LAZY BOOKWORMS!

WHAT DO YOU CALL A DINOSAUR THAT IS SLEEPING BEAUTY?

A SLEEPY DINO-SNORE!

WHAT IS FAST, LOUD, NOISY AND CRUNCHY?

A ROCKET AND MISSILE CHIP!

WHY DID THE CUTE TEDDY BEAR SAY NO TO DESSERT?

BECAUSE SHE WAS HEAVILY STUFFED.

WHAT HAS BIG EARS BUT CANNOT HEAR?

A GREEN CORNFIELD.

WHAT DID THE LEFT ROUNDING EYE SAY TO THE RIGHT EYE?

BETWEEN US, SOMETHING SMELLS BAD!

WHAT DO YOU GET WHEN YOU CROSS A HORRIBLE VAMPIRE AND A SNOWMAN?

HUMID FROST BITE!

WHAT DID ONE PLATE SAY TO THE OTHER DUMB PLATE?

YUMMY DINNER IS ON ME!

WHY DID THE STUDENT EAT HIS DELICIOUS HOMEWORK?

BECAUSE THE TEACHER TOLD HIM IT WAS A PIECE OF CHOCOLATE CAKE!

WHEN YOU LOOK FOR SOMETHING SPECIAL, WHY IS IT ALWAYS IN THE LAST PLACE YOU LOOK?

BECAUSE WHEN YOU FIND IT, YOU STOP LOOKING FOR ANYTHING.

WHAT IS BROWN, HAIRY, STYLISH AND WEARS SUNGLASSES?

A COCONUT ON LOOOONG VACATION.

TWO PICKLES FELL OUT OF A JAR ONTO THE MIRROR FLOOR. WHAT DID ONE SAY TO THE OTHER?

DILL WITH IT PLAY WITH IT.

WHAT DID THE DALMATIAN SAY AFTER SLOW LUNCH?

THAT HIT THE PROMINENT SPOT!

WHY DID THE FAST KID CROSS THE PLAYGROUND?

TO GET TO THE OTHER MUDDY SLIDE.

HOW DOES A DARK VAMPIRE START A LETTER?

BIG TOMB IT MAY CONCERN...

WHAT DO YOU CALL A DROID THAT TAKES THE LONG WAY AROUND OTHER?

R2 DETOUR.

How do you stop an astronaut's baby from crying and frying?

You fast rocket!

Why was one 6 afraid of two 7?

Because 7, 8, 9 each other

What is a witch's favorite subject in other school?

Hard Spelling!

When does a joke become a "dad and mom" joke?

When the punchline is a sweet parent.

How do you make a sour lemon drop?

Just let it fall down.

What did the limestone say to the genius geologist?

Don't take me for dirty granite!

What do you call a bright duck that gets all A's?

A wise and quick quacker.

Why does a seagull fly over the deep sea?

Because if it flew over the long bay, it would be a baygull.

WHAT KIND OF CLEAR WATER CANNOT FREEZE?

HOT WATER FREEZING WATER.

WHAT KIND OF TREE FITS IN YOUR SMALL HAND?

A BIG PALM TREE!

WHY DID THE SICK COOKIE GO TO THE HOSPITAL?

BECAUSE HE FELT CRUMMY AND DUMPY.

WHY WAS THE BABY STRAWBERRY CRYING RED TEARS?

BECAUSE HER MOM AND DAD WERE IN A STICKY JAM.

WHAT DID THE LITTLE CORN SAY TO THE SWEET MAMA CORN?

WHERE IS OTHER POP CORN?

WHAT IS WORSE THAN RAINING CATS AND DOGS EVERYTIME?

HAILING TAXIS!

HOW MUCH DOES IT COST A PIRATE TO GET HIS BIG EARS PIERCED?

ABOUT A BUCK AN EAR.

WHERE WOULD YOU FIND AN ELEPHANT FOR BEHIND MOUSE?

THE SAME PLACE AS YOU LOST HER ON OTHER SIDE!

HOW DO YOU TALK TO A HORRIBLE GIANT?

USE BIG WORDS AND SENTENCE!

WHAT ANIMAL IS ALWAYS BEST AT A BASEBALL GAME?

A FLYING BAT.

WHAT FALLS IN COLD WINTER BUT NEVER GETS HURT?

COTTON SNOW!

WHAT DO YOU CALL A BLACK GHOST'S TRUE LOVE?

HIS GHOUL-FRIEND LOVE.

WHAT BUILDING IN NEW YORK HAS THE MOST INTERESTING STORIES?

THE PUBLIC LIBRARY AT BIG SPOT!

WHAT DID ONE VOLCANO SAY TO THE OTHER AT SAME TIME?

I LAVA YOU I MASS YOU!

HOW DO WE KNOW THAT THE OCEAN IS FRIENDLY AND LOVELY?

IT WAVES BEAUTIFULLY!

WHAT IS A BIG TORNADO'S FAVORITE GAME TO PLAY?

TWISTER FISTER!

HOW DOES THE MOON CUT HIS CURLY HAIR?

ECLIPSE IT STRAIGHT IT.

HOW DO YOU GET A SHARP SQUIRREL TO LIKE YOU?

ACT LIKE A ROUND NUT!

WHAT DO YOU CALL TWO SMALL BIRDS IN LOVE?

TWEETHEARTS AND LOVELY!

HOW DOES A MAD SCIENTIST FRESHEN HER BREATH?

WITH CRAZY EXPERI-MINTS!

HOW ARE FALSE SMALL TEETH LIKE STARS?

THEY COME OUT AT BLACK NIGHT!

HOW CAN YOU TELL A FLYING VAMPIRE HAS A COLD?

SHE STARTS COFFIN SUDDENLY.

WHAT'S WORSE THAN FINDING A WORM IN YOUR FAVOURITE APPLE?

FINDING HALF A WORM.

WHAT IS A COMPUTER'S FAVORITE SNACK EVERYTIME?

COMPUTER CHIPS LIKE LAYS!!

WHY DON'T ELEPHANTS CHEW EVERY GUM?

THEY DO, JUST NOT IN PUBLIC DUE TO SHY.

WHAT WAS THE FIRST ANIMAL IN SPACE EVERYTIME?

THE BIG COW THAT JUMPED OVER THE MOON

WHAT DID THE BANANA SAY TO THE BARKING DOG?

NOTHING. BANANAS CAN'T TALK AND BARK.

WHAT TIME IS IT WHEN THE ROOM CLOCK STRIKES 13?

TIME TO GET A NEW NICE CLOCK.

HOW DOES A CUCUMBER BECOME A OILY PICKLE?

IT GOES THROUGH A JARRING BAD EXPERIENCE.

WHAT DO YOU CALL A PLAYING BOOMERANG THAT WON'T COME BACK?

A WANDERED STICK.

WHAT DO YOU THINK OF THAT NEW CANDLE LIGHT DINER ON THE MOON?

FOOD WAS GOOD, BUT THERE REALLY WASN'T MUCH BREATHING ATMOSPHERE.

WHY DID THE DINOSAUR CROSS THE CROWDY ROAD?

BECAUSE THE BAD CHICKEN WASN'T BORN YET.

WHY CAN'T ELSA HAVE A WHITE BALLOON?

BECAUSE SHE WILL LET IT GO AGAIN.

HOW DO YOU MAKE AN OCTOPUS LAUGH AND ROLLING?

WITH TEN-TICKLES AND NINE-PICKLES!

HOW DO YOU MAKE A SOFT TISSUE DANCE?

YOU PUT A LITTLE BOOGIE IN IT AND MAKE IT DANCING DOLL.

WHAT'S GREEN AND CAN FLY AND RUN?

SUPER DUPER PICKLE!

Knock knock tick tock.

Who's there? Who is coming?

Interrupting piratee.

Interrupting pir—*YARRRRRR!*

What did the nose say to the fluffy finger?

Quit picking on me and go!

What musical instrument is found in the dirty bathroom?

A tuba toothpaste and brush.

Why did the kid bring a long ladder to school?

Because she wanted to go to high school secretly.

WHAT IS A BLOODY VAMPIRE'S FAVORITE FRUIT?

A BLOOD ORANGE AND RED MANGO.

WHAT DO ELVES LEARN IN OTHER SCHOOL?

THE SINGING ELF-ABET.

WHAT DO YOU CALL A BARKING DOG MAGICIAN?

A LABRACADABRADOR.

WHERE DO SHARP PENCILS GO ON VACATION?

PENCIL-VANIA MANIA.

WHY COULDN'T THE MONY PONY SING A LULLABY?

SHE WAS A LITTLE MORE HOARSE

WHY DIDN'T THE ALONE SKELETON GO TO THE DANCE?

HE HAD NO BODY TO DO DANCE WITH.

WHAT GETS WETTER THE MORE IT DRIES SOMETIMES?

A DECENT TOWEL.

WHAT DO YOU CALL TWO ALONE BANANAS?

RAINY SLIPPERS.

WHY DID THE BANANA GO TO THE FOOLISH DOCTOR?

BECAUSE IT WASN'T PEELING WELL FASTLY.

WHAT DO YOU CALL A FAKE SOFT NOODLE?

A YUMMY IMPASTA.

WHAT STAYS IN THE CORNER YET CAN TRAVEL ALL OVER THE ROUNDED WORLD?

AN OLD STAMP.

HOW DO YOU FIX A CRACKED BIG PUMPKIN?

WITH A PUMPKIN PATCH ATTACHED.

WHAT KIND OF DESERVING AWARD DID THE DENTIST RECEIVE?

A LITTLE PLAQUE IN TEETH.

WHAT DO YOU CALL A FUNNY DANCING MOUNTAIN?

HILL-ARIOUS AND ROCKING.

WHY ARE GOOD GHOSTS BAD LIARS?

BECAUSE YOU CAN SEE RIGHT THROUGH THEM IN WRONG WAY.

WHY DO HONEY BEES HAVE STICKY HAIR?

BECAUSE THEY USE A HONEYCOMB OFTEN.

WHAT DID THE BIG FLOWER SAY LOUDLY TO THE LITTLE FLOWER?

HI, BUD WHAT'S UP!

WHY WAS THE PICTURE SENT TO DARK JAIL?

IT WAS FRAMED RAPIDLY.

WHERE DO CUTE RABBITS GO AFTER THEY GET MARRIED?

ON A BUNNY-MOON SOON!

WHAT SOUND DO PORCUPINES MAKE WHEN THEY HUG TIGHTLY?

OUCH!

WHY DO SHARP DUCKS MAKE GREAT DETECTIVES?

THEY ALWAYS QUACK THE CASE AND FACE.

WHAT DID ONE BIG WALL SAY TO THE OTHER SMALL WALL?

I'LL MEET YOU AT THE SMALL CORNER.

WHAT DO GENIUS LAWYERS WEAR TO COURT?

LAWSUITS AND ROOTS TO COURT.

WHAT KIND OF HAIR DO BIG OCEANS HAVE?

WAVY AND DEEP.

WHAT'S BLACK & WHITE AND READ ALL OVER AND OVER?

A PAGE TO PAGE NEWSPAPER. (OKAY, THIS ONE MIGHT REQUIRE AN EXPLANATION FOR DIGITAL-AGED KIDS).

AND, WHAT IS BLACK, WHITE, PINK AND GREEN ALL OVER?

A MANGO PICKLE IN A TUXEDO.

WHAT TIME IS IT IF AN ELEPHANT SITS ON THE TOUCHING FENCE?

TIME TO FIX THE HURTING FENCE!

WHAT PART OF YOUR BODY CAN CAUSE THE END OF THE ROUND WORLD?

YOUR APOCO-LIPS (AJ, AGE 8!)

WHAT DO YOU CALL AN OLD MODERN SNOWMAN?

WATER AND FIRE.

WHY DIDN'T THE ONE ORANGE WIN THE RACE?

IT RAN OUT OF JUICE AND FALL ASLEEP.

WHAT DINOSAUR HAD THE BEST AND TOUGH VOCABULARY?

THE THESAURUS.

WHAT DID ONE SMALL DNA STRAND SAY TO THE OTHER BIG DNA STRAND?

DO THESE GENES MAKE MY BUTT LOOK BIG AND HUGE?

WHY AREN'T GOOD DOGS GOOD DANCERS?

THEY HAVE TWO LEFT FEET AND ONE NECK.

WHAT DID THE HORRIBLE WOLF SAY WHEN IT STUBBED ITS TOE?

OWWWWW-CH!

KID: WHAT ARE YOU DOING UNDER THERE SINCE LAST NIGHT?

MOM: UNDER WHERE?

KID: HA HA! YOU SAID UNDERWEAR!!

WHY DID JOHNNY THROW THE CLOCK OUT OF THE MIRROR WINDOW?

BECAUSE HE WANTED TO SEE TIME FLY LIKE A BEE.

WHAT DID ONE DIRTY TOILET SAY TO THE OTHER?

YOU LOOK FLUSHED ALL TIME.

WHY DID THE MAN PUT HIS MONEY IN THE COLD FREEZER?

HE WANTED COLD HARD CASH RUNNING ALL TIME!

Q: **WHAT DOES A NOSEY MOZZY PEPPER DO?**

A: GETS JALAPENO BUSINESS DONE!

Q: **WHAT DO YOU CALL A FAKE CURLY NOODLE?**

A: AN IMPASTA

Q: WHAT DO YOU CALL AN ALLIGATOR IN A VEST AT OTHER TIME?

A: AN INVESTIGATOR INVESTING SERIOUSLY

Q: WHAT HAPPENS IF YOU EAT YEAST AND SHOE POLISH STEADILY?

A: EVERY MORNING YOU'LL RISE AND SHINE LIKE POLISH!

Q: "WHAT'S THE DIFFERENCE BETWEEN A GUITAR IN SHOP AND A FISH IN WATER?"

A: "YOU CAN'T TUNA FISH SWEETLY."

Q: DID YOU HEAR ABOUT THE RACE BETWEEN THE LETTUCE AND THE RED TOMATO?

A: THE LETTUCE WAS A "HEAD" AND THE RED TOMATO WAS TRYING TO "KETCHUP"!

Q: WHAT IS IT CALLED WHEN A BLUE EYED CAT WINS A DOG SHOW?

A: A CAT-HAS-TROPHY!

Q: WHY CAN'T YOU GIVE ELSA A RED BALLOON?

A: BECAUSE SHE WILL LET IT GO AND IT WILL BLAST.

Q: WHAT DO YOU GET FROM A PAMPERED FAT COW?

A: SPOILED MILK.

Q: WHAT DO LAWYERS WEAR TO EVERY COURT?

A: EVERY LAWSUITS!

Q: WHAT GETS SUDDEN WETTER THE MORE IT DRIES?

A: A DECENT TOWEL.

Q: WHAT DO YOU GET IF YOU CROSS A LIGHT CAT WITH A DARK HORSE?

A: KITTY PERRY FAIRY

Q: WHAT DID THE PENCILE SAY TO THE OTHER SMALL PENCIL?

A: YOUR LOOKING SHARP AND SMART.

Q: WHAT DID BACON SAY TO RED TOMATO?

A: LETTUCE GET TOGETHER IN A RALLY!

Q: WHAT IS THE MOST HARDWORKING PART OF THE HUMAN EYE?

A: THE PUPIL

Q: HOW DO YOU MAKE A HARD TISSUE DANCE?

A: PUT A LITTLE BOOGEY IN IT!

Q: WHY DID THE PICTURE GO TO DARK JAIL?

A: BECAUSE IT WAS FRAMED ACCURATELY.

Q: WHAT DO YOU CALL INNOCENT SECURITY GUARDS WORKING OUTSIDE SAMSUNG SHOPS?

A: GUARDIANS OF THE GALAXY WORLD.

Q: WHAT DO YOU GET WHEN YOU CROSS MOUSE LIKE FISH AND AN ELEPHANT?

A: SWIMMING TRUNKS WITH GIANTS.

Q: WHERE DO HONEY BEES GO TO THE BATHROOM?

A: AT THE BP STATION!

Q: WHAT DO YOU CALL A BABY MONKEY FUNKEY?

A: A CHIMP OFF THE OLD BLOCK ROAD.

Q: WHO EARNS A LIVING DRIVING THEIR LOYAL CUSTOMERS AWAY?

A: A TAXI DRIVER DRIVING CYCLE.

Q: "HOW DO YOU SHOOT A HORRIBLE KILLER BEE?"

A: "WITH A BEE BEE GUN."

Q: HOW DO YOU DROWN A SHINING HIPSTER?

A: IN THE MAINSTREAM.

Q: HOW DO YOU MAKE OTHER HOLY WATER?

A: BOIL THE HELL OUT OF IT AND RUN!

Q: WHAT HAPPENED TO THE AFRAID DOG THAT SWALLOWED A FIREFLY?

A: IT BARKED WITH DE-LIGHT!

Q: What stays in the corner and travels all over the round world?

A: A stamp.

Q: Why did the genius computer go to the doctor?

A: Because it had a severe virus!

Q: Why are jumping frogs so happy?

A: They eat whatever bugs them and so on

Q. What do you get when you cross a cow and a white duck?

A. Milk and quackers!

Q: WHAT DID THE ROARING LEOPARD SAY AFTER EATING HIS OWNER?

A: MAN, THAT HIT THE "SPOT."

Q: WHAT DO YOU CALL A SLEEPING LAZY BULL?

A: A LAZY BULLDOZER!

Q: WHAT IS THE TALLEST BUILDING IN THE WORLD AROUND?

A: THE BOOK LIBRARY! IT HAS THE MOST STORIES!

Q: WHAT DO YOU CALL A BELT WITH A TIME WATCH ON IT?

A: A WAIST OF TIME EVERY TIME

Q: WHY DID THE STUPID BANANA HAVE TO SEE THE DOCTOR?

A: BECAUSE IT WAS NOT PEELING VERY WELL

Q: WHY IS COOL ENGLAND THE WETTEST COUNTRY?

A: BECAUSE THE GORGEOUS QUEEN HAS REIGNED THERE FOR YEARS!

Q: WHY DO SMALL FISH LIVE IN SALT WATER?

A: BECAUSE PEPPER MAKES THEM SNEEZE ABRUPTLY!

Q: WHY DID THE MAN PUT HIS MONEY IN THE DEEP FREEZER?

A: HE WANTED COLD HARD CASH!

Q: WHAT DO YOU GET WHEN YOU CROSS A SOBER SNOWMAN WITH A DEVIL VAMPIRE?

A: FROSTBITE.

Q: WHAT IS THE BEST DAY TO GO TO THE SUMMER BEACH?

A: SUNDAY, OF COURSE!

Q: WHAT LITTLE BOW CAN'T BE TIED?

A: A SHINNING RAINBOW!

Q: WHAT OTHER SEASON IS IT WHEN YOU ARE ON A TRAMPOLINE?

A: SPRING FRINGE TIME.

Q: WHERE DID THE COMPUTER GO TO DANCE AT NIGHT?

A: TO A DISC-O LETS GO.

Q: WHAT HAS ONE HEAD, ONE FOOT AND FOUR LEGS?

A: A BED

Q: WHAT IS THE DIFFERENCE BETWEEN A SCHOOL TEACHER AND A FAST TRAIN?

A: THE TEACHER SAYS SPIT YOUR STICKY GUM OUT AND THE TRAIN SAYS "CHEW CHEW CHEW".

Q: WHY DID THE BIRDIE GO TO THE NEARBY HOSPITAL?

A: TO GET A TWEETMENT FOR WELLNESSSSS.

Q: WHAT DO YOU CALL SOMEONE WHO IS AFRAID OF SANTA BABA?

A: A CLAUSTERPHOBIC

Q: WHAT SOUND DO PORCUPINES MAKE WHEN THEY KISS SUDDENLY?

A: OUCH

Q: WHY WAS THE GUY LOOKING FOR FAST FOOD ON HIS FRIEND LUNCH?

A: BECAUSE HIS FRIEND SAID DINNER IS ON ME.

Q: WHY IS A 2017 CALENDAR MORE POPULAR AND VIRAL THAN A 2018 CALENDAR?

A: IT HAS MORE DATES AND MONTHS.

Q: DID YOU HEAR THE JOKE ABOUT THE ROOF TOP?

A: NEVER MIND, IT'S OVER YOUR HEAD AND FEET!

Q: WHAT IS BROWN AND HAS A HEAD AND A TAIL BUT NO LEGS AT ALL?

A: A PENNY.

Q: WHY DIDN'T THE SKELETON GO TO THE SCHOOL DANCE?

A: BECAUSE HE HAD NO-BODY TO GO WITH.

Q: HOW DO CRAZY PEOPLE GO THROUGH THE HORRIBLE FOREST?

A: THEY TAKE THE CONFUSING PSYCHO PATH.

Q: WHAT THREE CANDIES CAN YOU FIND IN EVERY HIGH SCHOOL?

A: NERDS, DUMDUMS, MARS AND SMARTIES.

Q: WHY ARE PIRATES CALLED PIRATES?

A: CAUSE THEY ARRRRR.

Q: WHAT DO INNOCENT PRISONERS USE TO CALL EACH OTHER?

A: A RINGING CELL PHONES.

Q: WHERE DO GENTLE SNOWMEN KEEP THEIR MONEY?

A: IN SNOW BANKS GENTLY.

Q: WHAT WASHES UP ON VERY SMALL SUMMER BEACHES?

A: UNCONTROLLABLE MICROWAVES!

Q: WHAT GOES THROUGH TOWNS, UP & OVER HILLS, BUT DOESN'T MOVE?

A: THE HILLY ROAD!

Q: WHY WAS THERE THUNDER AND LIGHTNING IN THE COMPUTER LAB?

A: THE INTELLIGENT SCIENTISTS WERE BRAINSTORMING!

Q: WHY DID SMALL TONY GO OUT WITH A PRUNE?

A: BECAUSE HE COULDN'T FIND A DATE AND A DAY!

Q: WHAT DID THE LITTLE BLACK MOUNTAIN SAY TO THE BIG MOUNTAIN?

A: HI CLIFF!

Q: WHAT DID WINNIE THE POOH SAY TO HIS AGENT SO SWEETLY?

A: SHOW ME THE HONEY PLEASEEE!

Q: WHAT DO YOU CALL A FUNNY ROCKING MOUNTAIN?

A: HILL-ARIOUS FABULOUS

Q: WHAT DID THE CANDLE SAY TO THE OTHER BURNING CANDLE?

A: I'M GOING OUT TONIGHT IN COOL BREEZE.

Q: WHY COULDN'T THE PIRATE PLAY CARDS SWEETLY?

A: BECAUSE HE WAS SITTING ON THE DECK!

Q: WHAT DID THE JANITOR SAY WHEN HE JUMPED OUT OF THE BIG CLOSET?

A: (SUPPLIES!)

Q: WHY DID THE TRAFFIC LIGHT TURN RED INSTEAD OF GREEN?

A: YOU WOULD TOO IF YOU HAD TO CHANGE IN THE MIDDLE OF THE STREET AT NIGHT!

Q: WHAT DID ONE SMALL ELEVATOR SAY TO THE OTHER ELEVATOR?

A: I THINK I'M COMING DOWN WITH SOMETHING LOADED!

Q: WHAT DO YOU SAY WHEN YOU LOSE AGAIN A WII GAME?

A: I WANT A WII-MATCH BIG MATCH!

Q: WHAT NEVER ASKS QUESTIONS BUT RECEIVES A LOT OF ANSWERS AT ANY TIME ANYWHERE?

A: THE RINGING TELEPHONE.

Q: HOW DO YOU MAKE AN OCTUPUS LAUGH AND TALK?

A: WITH TEN-TICKLES

Q: WHY CAN'T YOUR NOSE BE 12 INCHES LONG AND FAT?

A: BECAUSE THEN IT WOULD BE A FOOT!

Q: WHAT HAS FOUR WHEELS AND FLIES ON IT?

A: A GARBAGE TRUCK ON ROAD!

Q: WHAT STARTS WITH A P, ENDS WITH AN E, AND HAS A MILLION LETTERS IN IT FIX AT A SPOT?

A: POST OFFICE!

Q: WHAT DID THE WARM BLANKET SAY TO THE BED?

A: DON'T WORRY, I'VE GOT YOU COVERED COMPLETELY!

Q: WHY SHOULD YOU TAKE A SHARP PENCIL TO BED?

A: TO DRAW THE SHINY CURTAINS!

Q: HOW MANY INTERESTING BOOKS CAN YOU PUT IN AN EMPTY BACKPACK?

A: ONE! AFTER THAT ITS NOT EMPTY!

Q: WHAT KIND OF RED FLOWER DOESN'T SLEEP AT NIGHT?

A: THE DAY-ZZZ

Q: DID YOU HEAR THEY'RE CHANGING THE MIRROR FLOORING IN DAYCARE CENTERS?

A: THEY'RE CALLING IT INFANT-TILE!

Q: WHAT KIND OF SOFT BUTTON WON'T UNBUTTON?

A: A BELLYBUTTON!

Q: WHAT DID THE WHITE TRIANGLE SAY TO THE BLACK CIRCLE?

A: YOUR POINTLESS!

Q: WHY DO SEA-GULLS FLY OVER THE HUGE SEA?

A: BECAUSE IF THEY FLEW OVER THE BAY THEY WOULD BE BAGELS!

Q: WHAT PUNCTUAL DOG KEEPS THE BEST TIME?

A: A WATCH DOG.

Q: WHAT DID THE MAN SAY TO THE HARD WALL?

A: ONE MORE CRACK LIKE THAT AND I'LL PLASTER YA!

Q: WHY DID THE GREEN TOMATO TURN RED?

A: IT SAW THE SALAD DRESSING AND GOT SHY!

Q: WHY DO GIRLS SCOUTS SELL COOKIES IN STREET?

A: THEY WANNA MAKE A SWEET AND SOUR FIRST IMPRESSION.

Q: WHAT DID THE YELLOW GRAPE DO WHEN IT GOT STEPPED ON?

A: IT LET OUT A LITTLE WINE IN GLASS!

Q: WHAT KIND OF BERRY HAS A COLORING BOOK IN HIS ROOM?

A: A CRAYON-BERRY ROOMY

Q: WHAT DID THE ANGRY JUDGE SAY WHEN THE SKUNK WALKED IN THE COURT ROOM?

A: FEELING ODOR IN THE COURT.

Q: WHAT DID THE SMALL FISH SAY WHEN HE SWAM INTO THE WALL?

A: DAM!

Q: WHY DON'T SKELETONS FIGHT EACH OTHER WHEN THEY WANT?

A: THEY DON'T HAVE THE DECENT GUTS.

Q: WHAT DID THE JANITOR SAY WHEN HE JUMPED OUT OF THE SMALL CLOSET?

A: SUPPLIES!

Q: WHY DID THE GENIUS SCIENTIST GO TO THE TANNING SALON?

A: BECAUSE HE WAS A FOOL PALEONTOLOGIST.

Q: WHY DID THE ORANGE STOP RUNNING?

A: BECAUSE HE RAN OUT OF JUICE!

Q: WHY DID THE BOY TIPTOE PAST THE MEDICINE CABINET?

A: HE DIDN'T WANT TO WAKE THE SLEEPING PILLS!

Q: WHAT DO YOU GET WHEN YOU CROSS A FRIDGE WITH A SIGNING RADIO?

A: COOL AND JAZZ MUSIC.

Q: WHAT GOES UP WHEN THE COOL RAIN COMES DOWN?

A: AN UMBRELLA.

Q: WHY DID THE BELT GO TO DARK JAIL?

A: BECAUSE IT HELD UP A PAIR OF PANTS HERE!

Q: WHAT HAPPENS IF LIFE GIVES YOU BIG MELONS?

A: YOUR DYSLEXIC

Q: WHAT DID THE STAMP SAY TO THE WHITE FOLDED ENVELOPE?

A: STICK WITH ME AND WE WILL GO PLACES TO ENJOY!

Q: WHAT KIND OF COLOURFUL LIGHTS DID NOAH USE ON THE ARK?

A: FLOOD BURNING LIGHTS!

Q: WHY DON'T YOU SEE BIG GIRAFFES IN ELEMENTARY SCHOOL?

A: BECAUSE THEY'RE ALL IN HIGH SCHOOL STUDYING GEOGRAPHY!

Q: WHICH IS THE OTHER LONGEST WORD IN THE DICTIONARY?

A: "SMILES", BECAUSE THERE IS A MILE BETWEEN EACH "S"!

Q: WHICH MONTH DO SOLDIERS HATE MOST IN TIME?

A: THE MONTH OF MARCH!

Q: What did the creative painter say to the wall?

A: One more crack like that and I'll plaster you madly!

Q: Why did the computer break up with the wide internet?

A: There was no "Connection" interfering.

Q: Why do golfers wear two pairs of tight pants?

A: In case they get a deep hole in one!

Q: Why can't you take a nap during a long race?

A: Because if you snooze, you loose like hare!

Q: WHY DID GOOFY PUT A CLOCK UNDER HIS WOODY DESK?

A: BECAUSE HE WANTED TO WORK OVER-TIME!

Q: WHY DID JOHNNY THROW THE CLOCK OUT OF THE MIRRORED WINDOW?

A: BECAUSE HE WANTED TO SEE TIME FLY IN SECONDS!

Q: WHAT DO YOU CALL A BOOK THAT'S ABOUT THE GENIUS BRAIN?

A: A MIND READER AND STREAMER.

Q: WHEN DO YOU STOP AT GREEN AND GO AT RED ON ROAD?

A: WHEN YOU'RE EATING A GREEN WATERMELON!

Q: Why did God make only one funny Yogi Bear?

A: Because when he tried to make a second one he made a Boo-Boo

Q: How did the hardworking farmer mend his pants?

A: With yummy cabbage patches!

Q: Why did the young man lose his job at the orange juice factory?

A: He couldn't concentrate any time!

Q: How do you repair a broken red tomato?

A: Tomato Paste curry!

Q: WHY DID THE BABY STRAWBERRY CRY WITH RED TEARS?

A: BECAUSE HIS PARENTS WERE IN A STICKY JAM!

Q: WHAT WAS THE BLACK CAT IN THE HAT LOOKING FOR IN THE TOILET?

A: FOR THING ONE AND THING TWO.

Q: WHAT DID THE HAMBURGER NAME HIS SWEET DAUGHTER?

A: PATTY FATTY!

Q: WHAT KIND OF EGG DID THE BAD LAZY CHICKEN LAY?

A: A DEVILED EGG!

Q: WHAT KIND OF KEY OPENS THE HARD DOOR ON THANKSGIVING?

A: A TURKEY!

Q: WHY DID THE CRUNCHY COOKIE GO TO THE HOSPITAL?

A: HE FELT CRUMMY AND YUMMY!

Q: WHY WERE THE TEACHER'S EYES CROSSED?

A: SHE COULDN'T CONTROL HER NAUGHTY PUPILS!

Q: WHAT DO YOU CALL A OPEN GUY WHO NEVER FARTS IN PUBLIC?

A: A PRIVATE SHY TUTOR.

Q: WHAT DO YOU CALL A BUNNY BEAR WITH NO SOCKS ON?

A: BARE-FOOT BUNNY BEAR.

Q: WHAT CAN YOU SERVE BUT NEVER EAT?

A: A VOLLEYBALL.

Q: WHAT KIND OF SOFT SHOES DO ALL SPIES WEAR?

A: FUNKY SNEAKERS.

Q: WHY DID THE SOCCER PLAYER BRING STRING TO THE OTHER GAME?

A: SO HE COULD TIE THE SCORE AT TOP.

Printed in Great Britain
by Amazon